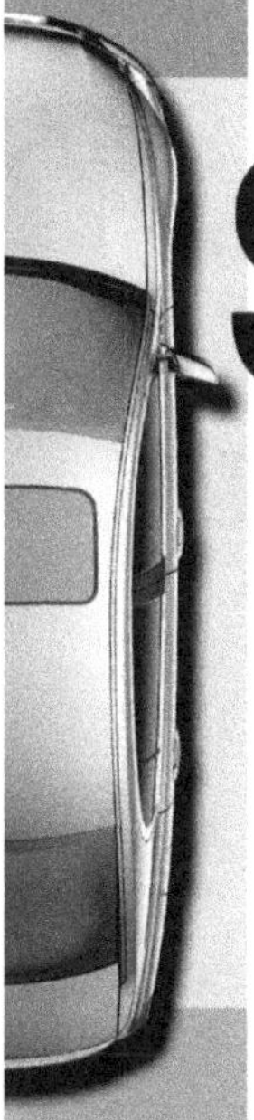

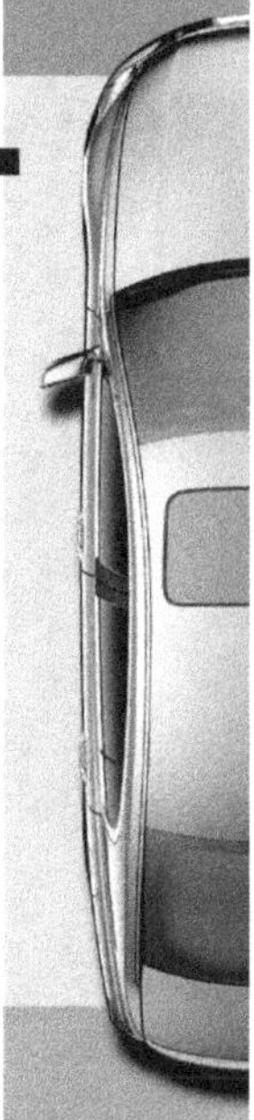

HOW

TO

START

AND

RUN

A

SUCCESSFUL
DRIVING
SCHOOL

Steven Trimble JD

HOW TO START AND RUN A SUCCESSFUL DRIVING SCHOOL

BY

Steven Trimble JD

CONTENTS

Chapter 1: Some History about the Industry

The United Kingdom started the driver education industry in 1909-1910, with the British School of Motoring founding a school in London (ca. 1910) by Hugh Stanley Roberts. It was geared towards hands on, behind-the-wheel driving skills and maintenance. Stateside, in the U.S., Amos Neyhart, a Penn State University professor, established the first course in driver education at State College High School in 1932 and taught the first driver education teacher prep course in driver education in 1936. Neyhart also wrote the first textbook on driver education, "The Safe Operation of an Automobile", published in 1934.

Fast forward to 1953 when Dr. George Hensel established the California Driving School in southern California and grew it to be one of America's largest driving schools and training facilities (25+ locations and over 100 cars). Hensel also founded the DSAA (Driving School Association of the Americas) in 1973 which is still active as of this writing, and serves over 6,000 driving schools. I had the good fortune to meet up with Dr. Hensel at DSAA conventions and consult with him whenever I needed expert advice. He was always amiable and willing to be of help. He was truly indeed a giant in the industry.

My beginnings were not quite as auspicious. I came into the industry in 1980 after being interviewed by my soon-to-be boss, Richard A. Jackson in Springfield, Ohio. At the time, Mr. Jackson had a chain of schools in the greater Dayton and Springfield area. It was a fateful meeting as I had responded to a blind help wanted ad for an office manager. Then I was trying to get back on my feet after returning from a short move to Phoenix. When I arrived at his office, I was surprised to see that it was a driving school. Knowing nothing about the business, besides being trained at a driving school as a teen, I made my way inside curious to see exactly what the job consisted of. As the interview began I sensed almost immediately that I wasn't what he was looking for in an office manager. It didn't take long for him to get to the point----He was looking for an Administrative Assistant (at this time also known as "secretary"). Nothing wrong with this, but I felt it was misleading to run the ad asking for an office manager, something I'd already had experience as in the hotel industry. By this point, I was beside myself. I had been looking for work for weeks, had come close to getting hired at other, well known brand companies, and this was the last straw. So I stood up, told Mr. Jackson that if he wanted a secretary then he should have advertised for one. I then proceeded to walk out. He spoke up as I reached the door and said that he was hiring driving instructors for the summer and if I was interested to let him know by tomorrow. I remember responding, "If you think that I'd ever teach beginners how to drive then you must be out of your mind". Talk about famous last words. After cooling off and sleeping on it, I called him back the next day and began my training the following week.

The training required by the state of Ohio, at the time, was only 40 clock hours and upon finishing I was licensed to teach in-car and in-class. Believe me when I say that I was nowhere near as prepared as I should've been. I had begun, unbeknownst to me, the start of a lifetime career.

Chapter 2: Do You Really Want To Own A Driving School?

Of course you do! Otherwise, why would you have purchased this book?! Right?! But let's give this a little more thought, shall we.

In my forty plus years of operating driving schools, I've met many people that wanted to own their own school. Unfortunately, many start out the wrong way. And the wrong way, as far as I'm concerned, is to go to work for a school owner as an instructor, learn the business, and upon learning how it operates, open up a school in the same area and then compete head to head with that owner who was kind enough to give them a job. At a minimum, it is disloyal, unethical, and an act of bad faith.

You may disagree and say that there's nothing wrong with the aforementioned scenario. After all, business is business. But let's look at it from a boss's perspective. He or she doesn't suspect that they're training a future competitor. Trade secrets, instruction techniques, valuable business contacts, et al, can all be shared by the boss, with a new hire, in good faith. So if you decide to learn the business in this way, at least be upfront with the owner and let him or her know your intentions. Why not? Does it mean that you'll be showing your hand? Well, yes it does. But it also shows that you will begin the business relationship working for them in good faith. They can teach you their methods of instruction and operations, but also keep other areas of the business private. Then if you do become a school owner in the same area, you both can be friendly competition, instead of vindictive and spiteful enemies.

Also, some see driver education as an opportunity to get rich quickly. They see how busy schools are during the summer and have visions of big money continuing year round. What they don't know is when football season starts and the student load dwindles down, they soon realize that the gold at the end of the rainbow is now further away. There is an ebb and flow to this business that must be planned for.

Remember that just because a business looks easy to run, doesn't mean that it is. Any successful business, that smoothly operates, has had its share of challenges. How ownership deals with challenges determines how well the business adjusts or pivots to function like a well oiled machine. If you learn nothing else from this chapter, understand that operating a driving school is far from easy. You can be firing on all cylinders (pun intended) and then a car or three breaks down. Or an instructor strikes another car and it's his or her fault. And you thought you only had to worry about students wrecking the cars?! This business is highly unpredictable, and after experiencing situations like I just described, you begin to appreciate just another uneventful, boring business day.

Furthermore, the personality and mindset of an owner must be such that you are able to handle many issues at once. From minor items: such as a student coming in too late to class, to major ones: such as going to an accident scene and helping shuttle an instructor and student/s to the emergency room to be evaluated after a crash. The public can be difficult to work with, students can be disrespectful, employees hard to manage, budgets busted due to a multitude of things that happen, and so on. You must learn to set aside your emotions and handle each and every situation logically and professionally; if for no other reason, than to maintain your own mental and emotional balance.

Lastly, don't think owning a driving school will be looked at and held in high regard. I can't tell you how many times I've been ridiculed, laughed at, insulted, patronized, talked down to, etc. In fact, I once had a sign behind my desk listing all the ways the public can be difficult to work with. It listed some of what I wrote above, and other sayings, and it said at the end, "The only reason I stay around this crazy place is to see what happens next!"

There are always two types of people that want to know who the owner is: Salespersons and upset parents of teen students. I will go into this in further detail in Chapter 4. Just realize that if you expect a favorable reaction when you tell others what you do for a living, it may be an underwhelming moment for you. Especially if you define yourself by your work.

So there you have it. If I haven't scared you off yet, then I guess you're ready to go forward in this career. My intentions are to simply be candid, let you know what you're getting yourself into, and make sure you proceed with eyes fully open.

Chapter 3: Setting Up and Launching Your School

First on the list is to choose a name for it that hasn't already been chosen by a currently licensed school. Try to come up with at least three or four names that you can live with. You want to also make sure that the name you choose is not deceptively similar to another operational school. Once that checks out, you then check your state's registered corporate names to confirm availability. Most likely if the name is already taken then both agencies will show this. It's certainly unusual if someone who's filed a corporation hasn't also filed with the state licensing agent too, but certainly not completely unheard of. Sometimes the applicant is either in the process of applying for a license (which would be purely coincidental) or they're using the corporation as a placeholder for a future school. Either way, it's just a lot easier if you go with another name. You don't want to get into a legal battle over naming rights before you've even begun.

NOTICE: I've already presumed that you will have chosen a corporation as the right business structure for your school. Have I known other owners that operated as a sole proprietor? Yes I have. But you must consider the liability involved and the potential for loss. Do you really want to risk your own personal assets with the possibility of a lawsuit? A corporation, whether a "C" corp, "S" corp, or LLC (limited liability corporation), will help protect everything you've worked hard for. And yes it's not completely foolproof. It's not impossible to "pierce the corporate veil". But it is less likely and does offer some degree of protection.

Next determine what courses you're going to offer and how you will offer them. Will you offer online classes or traditional bricks and mortar classes or both? Just starting out you may want to offer both since you're trying to establish your business (and brand). And the public, even though they've gotten progressively used to dealing with online providers, generally feels a little more comfortable if you have a physical location. This has certainly changed some since the pandemic but there are some people that still prefer to deal face to face.

NOTE: The public, before anything else, wants *comfort and convenience*.... especially when it comes to driver education. The easier you make it on them for their teen to attend your classes, the more appealing your school will be. For example: Consider offering a pickup service from school or home. You can also charge extra for this service and a plus to this is having your signed car seen at the local high school campus or neighborhood and advertising for you.

When choosing a location to operate out of, there are many things you need to do in advance of opening. If you're building is in the city you'll probably need to obtain a certificate of occupancy. A city inspector will visit onsite and make sure the site adheres to city code. I once had a school in the city that required an additional restroom. The inspector came in and immediately told me that I needed a male and female restroom. The restroom that I currently had was fine for women (one toilet and one sink) but another restroom must be added for the men that included a urinal and a toilet. At the time, that additional build-out cost $10k. That was an extra $10k I hadn't planned on spending.

Another inspection you'll need to have is a fire inspection. Regardless, of where you're located, as long as you are open to the public, this must be done. In the process of expanding into the county, the place I had selected had no back door exit. When the fire marshal came he told me that I needed a back door exit installed before he would approve the business. After appealing to the landlord and property owners, they insisted that would be my responsibility. So, again I spent a few thousand dollars to comply with the fire code.

Also from that point forward, I had to have a natural gas line check on the entire property for my annual license renewal. Guess what? I didn't have natural gas in my space nor was it necessary to conduct my business. But there was a restaurant in the center that used natural gas and I had to pay for his water heater modification, so the plumber that was hired would sign off on the natural gas line check. Again, more money spent over budget.

So why did I tell you all this? In the excitement of opening a business or expanding, it's easy to overlook key things. Don't learn the hard way. If you do your due diligence when looking for a spot to open, you can save yourself a lot of surprises and money.

Select a car or cars to be used. You'll want to start out with a small to midsized sedan, preferably a 4 door (back seat for observers). Make sure it's easy to drive and that bigger teens can fit in behind the wheel and also in the backseat, so "observers" in the back can see, be comfortable, and enter and exit the vehicle without incident. See chapter 7 for greater detail regarding this topic.

You will also want to have a bookkeeping/accounting system in place, a CPA or enrolled agent to make sure your taxes are done properly and offer you advice when you need it; an attorney that works primarily with small businesses (consider someone new to practicing law that needs clients and will want to see your business grow); and an insurance broker that is knowledgeable about the driving school industry. You want someone, preferably a one or two person firm, that has experience, but also is hungry for new clients and as you grow, you can grow with them. Professionals, such as CPA's and Attorneys, will continuously raise their fees as they gain experience and become more known in their field. Your goal is to strike a balance by making sure you get the proper attention you deserve and value for the money you spend for their services. If they help you make more money and/or protect what you've earned you'll gladly stay and grow with them. Remember that you're in this for the long haul.

Chapter 4: Personnel

You can name any type of customer oriented employee (aka associate) that there is or ever has been (except health care worker), and I've probably had them work for me. From GED to PhD, from young teens to seniors, from bad to good, I've had them all. Hiring, of course, was the easy part. It was always difficult though to figure out if they'd become a star performer. And sometimes, when they weren't a good fit, we would have to part ways. Letting someone go is never easy. This is why it's key to know what you're looking for in an employee and not settle for less.

When in need of an instructor, I tried multiple ways of recruiting them: Newspaper ads (when people actually read a newspaper), local school bulletin boards, street marquee signs, offers of a bonus to current employees, etc. But what often worked best were recommendations from current instructors. Now certainly when you're first getting started, you don't have that option, and you have to use multiple ways of getting the word out that you need help. And with the internet and social media you can spread the word, usually easier and cheaper than back in the day. So this can be a "pro" to finding instructors. A "con" would be that it's still a shotgun approach with varying levels of success. So after I hired my first group of instructors, trained them in the way I wanted them to teach, making sure they performed well enough to retain them after a trial period; I would then offer them a bonus ($100 at the time) to recruit someone they knew and would recommend. Of course, anyone that came recommended would still have to pass the interview process, training, and stay with the school through at least a summer. Then, and only then, the bonus would be paid. Also, the good thing about this is that the staff instructor that recommended the prospective one would have a vested interest in that person's success. Of course, nothing is 100% certain but more times than not it worked.

Throughout the years, I would get drop-ins and drive bys of licensed instructors and prospective front office personnel too. People would notice the business or signed cars and wonder if we were hiring. Sometimes it was an instructor that taught for a competitor and they were simply testing the market to see what I, and probably other school owners, would offer them. I won't say that I never hired them, because I did, especially when I was desperate for help. But it rarely turned out well. Most, if not all, had a set way of teaching and even after training them in the way I wanted them to teach, they'd usually fall back into bad habits acquired in the past. Also, there was one type of instructor that we'll call Mr. or Ms. Jump Ship. He or she would constantly be looking for a better deal (more money, a better training car, etc.) so they'd move on, and as luck would have it, usually at the busiest times of the year.

NOTE: One thing I never did was hire a front office person this way. I would always hire someone new to the industry and train them in the business. This person had to be especially trustworthy, reliable, honest, have a good personality, be loyal, and have other good attributes. He or she would be privy to trade secrets and confidential information that competitors would like to know. Someone coming aboard from another school would know their secrets but I always thought that if they could leave them, they could leave me just as easily. Now that doesn't mean that my rookie hire couldn't leave me for a competitor, but it was less likely.

Trial periods: It's important to set a time period in which to evaluate your new hire and confirm if he or she is a good fit for your company. Three months is usually adequate time to judge whether you'll keep that new hire or not. Make certain, in writing and verbally, that this is addressed at the time you onboard them.

A Story about a bad choice of an Instructor:

I'd like to share with you a story about a fellow that called one day and subsequently came in for an interview. For the sake of the story we'll call him Don. Don was a retired teacher looking for extra income. When we first met he was dressed well with a collared shirt, tie and slacks. Don had experience and was anxious to get started. So since I had a need for in-car instructors, I welcomed him aboard, and began to train him like I do all instructors, experienced or not, in the way I wanted him to teach. We went over all our routes and the in-car curriculum. Satisfied that he understood how to conduct lessons, I assigned him a car and his own student load.

We had just started into our summer season, and if you don't know by now this is always the busiest season in driver education. With his freshly assigned car and students, Don began his daily regimen of training novice student drivers. He began by taking the students to a residential area nearby to work on stops and starts, turns, lane changes, etc. And of course this is fine if the student is on their first or second lesson, but for whatever reason he seemed to always stay in the same neighborhood throughout most of the seven hours of lessons. Very little freeway driving was taught (and being near a major metropolitan area he knew that they'd be driving on the freeway a lot after getting their license), a cursory short lesson on parking, limited experience in city driving, and then to top it all off , he put the windows down and turned off the air conditioning in the heat of the summer! It being summer in Houston, it was very hot and humid. I have this mental picture of beet red-faced teens sweating in a hot car. It was beyond explanation...

But that's not all....

Since the property manager wouldn't allow me to keep my cars in the parking lot overnight, I'd allow my instructors to take the car home and park it in their driveway. This would keep the cars reasonably safe from getting broken into, vandalized or stolen. However, in Don's case, unbeknownst to me, he didn't have a paved driveway. So he would routinely park the training car on a dirt patch. Within a few weeks a large fire ant hill formed in the spot where he always parked the car. The ants began to crawl up into the engine compartment, fouling up the wiring, which then caused electrical problems After having it towed to my mechanic, he first had to eradicate the ants, take off the various wiring harnesses and rewire the damaged parts to one another. Upon completion of the job, which included him spending the entire weekend in the shop with wires looking like a bowl of spaghetti, and even taking it home to work on it, the mechanic told me that he'd never touch another car that Don was assigned to.

Bottom Line:

Vet all your instructors in the hiring process. The state usually has the applicant undergo a background check. But my background check not only included an FBI criminal check, but I usually had a private investigator run a separate check too. When you have someone working with minors you can't be too careful. And this is all well and good, but what if they pass their background check with flying colors but you still have someone like Don teaching in-car? Fortunately now there is an abundance of technology so you can monitor what's going on in the car at all times. Also, it doesn't hurt to do a spot check on the instructor's car occasionally. You can slowly start to trust them, but always take time to verify. Believe me when I say I learned a valuable lesson here with Don.

KEYPOINTS

Remember back in Chapter 2, I mentioned that there are two main types of people that want to know who the owner is? And those two types are parents of students and salespeople. Well, this is where personnel play a valuable part. Especially when it comes to complaints from an angry parent. If you hire well, complaints will be kept to a minimum regarding in-car and in-classroom instructors. And if your front desk person is trained properly to handle aggrieved customers, then this will take some of the burden off of you too. But, always follow up to make sure that everything was handled to their satisfaction. Most customers just want to be heard. So if you ignore them you do so at the risk of a bad online review and also bad word of mouth amongst their friends and family. If they have younger kids you stand to lose them too when they want to learn to drive.

And as far as salespeople go, they can be some of the biggest time wasters. If you're not interested, let them know right away. If on the phone, I always said something like, "Thank you for calling but it's just not something I'd be interested in. Have a good day". And then end the call. Some may think it's rude, but you're really doing them a favor. They can move on to the next person on their call list because they now know they haven't a chance making a sale with you.

Chapter 5: Training Your Instructors In-Car

Training your instructors for in-car instruction is literally where the rubber meets the road. If you rely on others to teach them, then you'll just end up with an instructor that uses a hodge-podge of instructional techniques that will undermine your best efforts to get the desired results from them. I'm certainly not saying that you can't hire an instructor that's worked for and been trained by someone else, but you absolutely must take them out on the road and demonstrate what order, how, and the why of your school's instruction techniques.

So, let's begin with your first in-car training with your freshly hired instructor. You'll work with them as you would any beginning driver so they can eventually mimic your technique. Starting with Lesson 1, Hour 1, you would demonstrate how to approach the car and do a walk around. Are the tires up? Is the car sitting level? Are there any fluids underneath the car? Clear liquid is okay (water condensation from AC), but colored liquid requires further inspection. Has the car been hit since it was parked? In a busy parking lot, this happens more than people realize. After this quick, 360 degree walk around, you then ask your trainee: How long did that take us? Most likely they'll say about 10-15 seconds. And this is probably the same response they'll get from a student when they do the same thing with him or her. It's here that you impress upon them the importance of doing this pre-check to avoid a problem or breakdown on the road. Better to learn about a problem first in a parking lot or driveway than on a busy road.

Next, you show your instructor, how to guide his/her student, in how to adjust the driver's seat. We use the acronym S.M.I.L.E.: S for seat, M for mirrors, I for interior, L for lights, and E for engage the engine (using key or key fob with button). Then you need to explain how to teach blind spots around the vehicle. Most of the public believes that there are only two (2) blind spots. But there really is at least 5 times that!

BLIND SPOTS

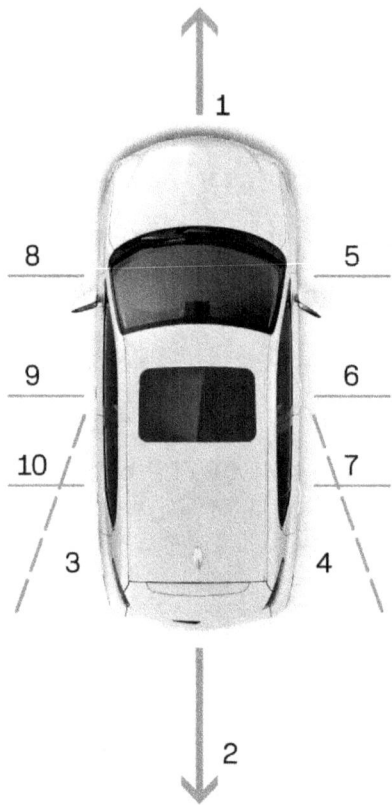

1. Front of vehicle
2. Back of vehicle
3. Left back side
4. Right back side
5. Right front A pillar
6. Right middle B pillar
7. Right back C pillar
8. Left front A Pillar
9. Left middle B Pillar
10. Left back C Pillar

Now, with the engine off, you will demonstrate how extensive the front and rear blind spots are. With the windows rolled down and the trainee behind-the-wheel, you'll tell him/her that you're going to walk out in front of the vehicle and walk backwards until they can see your feet on the pavement. As this happens, they are to wave out the window at you. Then you slowly walk forward until they see your feet disappear. At that point the trainee honks the horn. You then tell them to get out of the vehicle to see how much space was out of their field of vision.

This is especially important considering how tall pickup trucks have gotten. In fact, some pickups are so tall that a 7-8 year old child cannot be seen by a driver when they're directly in front of their truck.

You then perform the same demonstration from the rear of the vehicle with the trainee watching in the rearview mirror. This time, upon getting out of the car, they should see that it is much farther than what they'd witnessed in the front. This is when you explain that toddlers, pets, and even infants in carriers have been hit and run over by a rushed parent. Also, it's good to point out to not depend fully on cameras and the importance of the pre-drive check walk around.

NOTE: It is beyond the scope of this book to include hour by hour lessons. Depending on the state, you could be working with a teen student anywhere from 6-8 hours (or more) in-car. A curriculum may already be in place, but regardless you should be able to adapt it to what you feel is important to teach your students and instructors. If you want further, hour by hour, step by step instruction in-car, please consider checking out our 14 hour in-car curriculum. This was designed by myself and approved by the state of Texas, and it can be modified to fit state standards. You can contact us at betterdriving@peoplepc.com for further information.

Chapter 6: Training Classroom Instructors

"A good in-class instructor is worth their weight in gold."

And while you, as an owner, will probably insist on handling the classroom yourself in the beginning stages of your school; sooner or later you'll have to turn all classroom instruction over to competent teaching staff.

I have used a number of different in-class instructors over the years with varying results. As far as educational levels of staff went, they ran the gamut from GED to even a PhD. Regardless of how educated each instructor was, if they were trained properly and were sincere in learning the right way to teach driver education, they all had the potential to become a good to great instructor.

All classroom instructors should be supplied with the latest edition of teacher textbooks and curriculum, an up to date driver handbook, state traffic law manual, and state of the art audio visual aids. The students should have a laptop or pad to allow them to follow along with the teacher, to take notes or highlight certain areas, and take quizzes and tests as the classroom progresses.

Usually the first few hours of class are dedicated to teaching the students about road signs, signals, and traffic law and rules of the road. All states have a driver handbook (most are in PDF format), that the student can download and have offline access to both in-class and out. It's usually always a good idea to send each student a welcome email in advance of the start date with an attached handbook so they can begin skimming through it. Since time is always limited, it's important to cover the handbook completely; and since you certainly don't want to shortchange the student, the teen can then come to class with some knowledge about the subject matter.

In Texas, any school can conduct their training of instructors to comply with the requirements set by the legislature and regulated by the Texas Department of Licensing and Regulation (TDLR)— Driver Education and Safety Division. In other states it usually is overseen by the Department of Public Safety (DPS) or Department of Motor Vehicles (DMV). Depending on the owner and their choice of educational materials, the curriculum can vary from school to school. And it's not like you, as the owner, have to reinvent the wheel. There is curriculum already designed and ready to use, regardless of the state you're in, that is offered by major players in the industry (e.g. the American Automobile Association aka AAA). Always make sure that the program you choose is approved by the licensing agency your school is under. And certainly it would be advisable to research all programs to see if they would complement your style of teaching. Most will give you a free textbook to look over in hopes that they'll get a large order in return. Sometimes it's just mixing and matching to find out what works for you.

Also you can get a free download from the Association of National Stakeholders in Traffic Safety Education https://anstse.info/. This will include model curriculum to teach instructors in-classroom and in-car. It was assembled by a group of driving education and safety educators and curriculum writers that will give you a strong base of information to either build your own curriculum from or simply follow step-by-step.

KEY POINT---In training your instructors, you must KNOW YOUR STUFF. If your instructors know that you're knowledgeable then they'll respect you and be proud to work in your school. If you don't gain that respect from the beginning, you'll have an uphill battle and may never gain it. **You must always be the most knowledgeable instructor on your team.**

Chapter 7: Training Cars: Buying, Assigning and Maintaining

<u>Buying</u>

In choosing a training car there are several things to consider:

- Size of car
- Reliability
- Gas mileage or miles per charge
- Safety
- Ease of installing instructor brake (and maybe accelerator bar)
- Technology
- Is it easy for a novice driver to learn on?

The size of the car is important since you want to make sure that your students can fit in the rear seat for observation purposes (Texas requires observation time) or simply shuttling before or after their lesson. When looking for a vehicle make sure you sit in the backseat first, especially if you're fairly tall, to see if a big and tall teen can fit comfortably in the back.

If you're in the camp that only buys new vehicles, you will certainly want to vet and establish relations with new car dealers in your area. How long have they been in business? How are their reviews? Besides checking them out online, pay them a visit in person. There is no replacing seeing with your own two eyes, hearing how business is conducted, and getting an overall sense of how the dealership operates.

In buying cars, and I've bought new and used, I only deal with the fleet manager. After all, your goal is to one day have a fleet of cars on the road, even if you're only buying one now. There are four main reasons why you want to work with a fleet manager: (1) They usually will take more time with you, (2) They have a vested interest in establishing a long term business relationship with you, (3) You should get a better deal and (4) Should also have access to better vehicles than the general public (important if buying used).

Remember, you're not only starting a driving school but unintentionally now you're in the car business. Why do I say this? As you grow your fleet you'll be buying more vehicles, maintaining them, and squeezing as much life out of them as possible. How well you negotiate your deals and establish a pipeline for good reliable vehicles, will determine how much money you add to the bottom line. And when it's time for a vehicle replacement (or multiple), you want to have a fleet manager in place, ready to fill that need quickly and economically.

Assigning Vehicles

Until you get your team of instructors in place, you'll probably take a vehicle you own and turn it into a training car. Since you'll be the sole in-car instructor this would be prudent. As you begin to hire and train new instructors you can then buy a newer car (It does not have to be brand new), break in the newer car and pass down the older vehicle to your first hire. Then as you grow you simply duplicate the process. Eventually you will want and need to get off the road. So you would now begin to give the best vehicle to your instructor with the longest tenure and the older vehicles to the others in order of hire. The only time you would change this is if you are lucky enough to get a Star instructor.

Who is a Star instructor?

(1) They're reliable.

(2) They show up for appointments on time.

(3) You can trust them.

(4) They take exceptional care of their training car.

(5) They're requested by parents at sign up.

(6) It's more than just a job to them, so they perform their job very well.

(7) You know exactly what they're doing in-car and when they're doing it.

(8) And they let you know when something is wrong mechanically with the car.

This type of instructor you definitely want to keep happy and remain loyal. So as soon as you're able, you should upgrade his or her car. Not discounting the person with the longest tenure, and if they're both one and the same so much the better, but it's a key way to set yourself apart from your competition and incentivize other instructors to improve.

Maintaining Your Vehicles

Remember, that these vehicles are *your vehicles;* as much as the instructor may think otherwise (and I've had some instructors that believed that). In fact, I've had some instructors that carried so much stuff in the training car it looked like they lived out of it! But always remember and remind them that all of the vehicles belong to the company *and remember the company is you.*

It is vital to take care of your fleet. Even if it's only two cars, it is still a fleet, and deserves your undivided attention. Those cars, when running and on the road, are making you money. And by the same token, when a car or cars is in the shop it's costing you money. And if it's something that could've easily been avoided by routine maintenance then that's something that really affects your bottom line. This is why it's so important to impress upon your instructors the significance of routine maintenance and to let you know when they notice something wrong with the vehicle. I was a stickler for this and the instructors knew it. Of course, nobody will care for your vehicles like you do, and I understand that it's easy to rely on your instructors being vigilant with their vehicles, but believe me, it's rare when you have an instructor that takes care of your car like it was their own. So do a weekly check and a surprise walk around and test drive in between students to make sure the cars are well cared for. If you set up a foolproof system to never forget when maintenance is due, your cars will perform better, last longer, and with less *unforeseen* breakdowns.

Chapter 8: What To Do When Bad Things Happen

Sooner or later, something bad will happen. Murphy's Law will rear its ugly head. But if you prepare for it, it can be handled with the least amount of drama, inconvenience, and turmoil. The first thing to do is prepare a list of what could possibly go wrong. Then ask yourself: What can I do, right now, to head it off? For example, you know that one day, despite all precautions taken and your best efforts made, a student will wreck one of your training cars. What do you do right now to mitigate the expected effects of this? Because the chief objective is to mitigate impact to your students, your instructors, your school, and of course yourself. So taking our example you should:

- Go to the scene of the crash.
- Take lots of pictures from all angles.
- If an ambulance hasn't been called, call one. Have everyone you're responsible for checked at the scene or taken to the Emergency Room (ER).
- Call the parents of all students in the car and explain what has happened.
- Have parents meet up with you, and their teen, at the scene or ER.

- If it was a minor accident, and you've made absolutely certain that no one has been hurt (remember some effects from the collision won't show up until the next day or so), then offer to take the students home in your vehicle.

- Regardless, make certain that all insurance information, driver license info, VIN numbers, plate numbers are written down.

- Have students and instructor (if not hurt) write a statement explaining what they saw, heard or felt in the crash, while it's still fresh in their minds.

- If it's a major crash, call your insurance company and make a claim. If it's a minor one you might consider taking care of it out of pocket, depending on the circumstances. More about this later. (See "A Story")

If the car needs to be towed, do your best to make sure it's taken to a body shop or mechanic that you trust. Try not to let law enforcement give the car to any tow truck driver to take it to where they want it taken to. This can get very expensive quickly (i.e. towing charges, storage fees). Remember, the tow truck driver wants to make as much money as possible off your ill fortune. This means that the driver will take it to the shop that pays him a referral fee. So not only does the driver overcharge you for the tow but he gets a little something extra too. This is why you want to already have a good relationship established with an independent mechanic and body shop owner.

After everything has been done that you can possibly do, and things settle down, talk with your instructor to get his/her version of what happened. See if he or she tries to cover up mistakes that were made. Realize that everyone tries to paint themselves in the best light, and may not be completely truthful. So always take that into account. If you have a dash cam recording the incident, both inside and out, review it of course to make sure that everything, written or said, matches up. Preface the meeting by saying that you expect them to be totally truthful and if not there could be repercussions up to and including possible termination. And mean it. This is an area that you could potentially lose your school and livelihood in. And if you have an instructor that is incompetent and lies to you to cover up his or her mistakes, they have no business being an instructor, much less being under your employ.

A Srory

As I mentioned before, I would allow my instructors to take the training car home with them. My landlord wouldn't allow the fleet left overnight in the parking lot, and besides I'd worry about vandalism and theft during the night anyways. So it saved me from having to rent storage and saved the instructor time too. A win-win situation. Or so I thought.

One day I walked into the school and my assistant let me know that a fellow from the business across the street (a tint and auto stereo shop) had come by and wanted to talk to me. So I went over and he asked me to follow him to his brother's shop (a small engine repair place). Upon pulling up I noticed that one of the garage doors was smashed in. Well it didn't take much to put 2 and 2 together. Apparently, early that morning, my instructor had come by with his lawnmower to get it fixed. Evidently, he confused the accelerator and the brake, hit the accelerator, and smashed into the garage door. After looking at the damage on the outside, we then walked inside and saw how close the crushed garage door had come to a restored 1967 Cadillac Eldorado sitting inside. At that time it was probably worth over $20k. Having dodged a huge bullet, I told him to get an estimate on the door and I'd take care of it. Fortunately, the door wasn't as bad as it looked, but it still ended up costing me a few hundred dollars. At this point I seriously considered firing the instructor since he'd gone against company policy by using the car for his own errands. And my deductible was $1k anyway so it would've been useless to file a claim. So I had a long talk with him, warned him to never do it again (he had been a 5 year employee), and went on about our business, and never had a problem with him again.

KEY POINTS: To be prepared for the worst, you must have insurance, a team of professionals, and policies and procedures in place for the worst case scenarios. Your insurance will be a commercial policy with the highest amount you can afford. For example, I carried a million dollar policy because I sometimes had four people in-car and am in a state with lots of uninsured drivers. You must have workers compensation in the event that your employee is injured. Why? Because if you are in business long enough, one of your in-car instructors will get hurt and they'll make a claim. Without workers comp you may be forced to pay such a large claim that it could cause you to close down. You need general liability in the event that someone falls or hurts themselves in your place of business. Your team of professionals should include a CPA, Attorney, Insurance Broker or Agent, and bookkeeper (if you don't want to do the books yourself). You always want to stay in the good graces of the IRS. Note: A policy and procedure manual is a must for a driving school operation. The policy and procedure manual should be written by an attorney, with your input.

Chapter 9: Expanding Without Getting Too Big

When I first invested into the driving school industry , I bought into an established school with two locations. My objective was to expand the operation as large as possible across a major metropolitan area. This was the goal of the current president of the corporation, so we were certainly on the same page going forward.

Within two years we had opened up another storefront location and five years later we had a total of six. One would think that we were making a lot of money and everyone would be happy, right? Wrong! By this time we had lost one co-owner and every monthly meeting became a battleground as others that had bought in were trying to gain majority ownership. You see, when one person exited, the original owners bought their stock with company funds, and then resold the stock enriching themselves. This eventually led to the breakup of the corporation into three different corporations, with me and two others assuming the flagship and one expansion spot, and the other co-owners splitting up the other 4.

At the time, I was concerned and worried about what the future held. So in the next year, I dug in and worked even harder, splitting time between the two schools which were 25 miles apart. This may not sound far apart, but if you're instructing students daily: adults in the morning and early afternoon and weekends, teens after school and evenings, and driving all over the city, this got old fast.

Then to top it off, the state of Texas changed administrative agencies, from the DPS (Department of Public Safety) to the TEA (Texas Education Agency). And one of the new requirements for licensure of our flagship school in the city was to obtain a certificate of occupancy (COO). So dutifully, off I went to the building code inspection office to set up an onsite visit with an inspector. My partners had been in the same location for 16 years and never been required to go through such an inspection. When the inspector showed up he almost immediately went to the one bathroom and told me that we needed two separate bathrooms, male and female. In the men's bathroom a urinal and a toilet were required. The women's bathroom would be fine with one toilet. Until we remodeled (adding the men's bathroom) we would not be granted a COO. Of course this meant that we couldn't operate until this was taken care of. Two months shutdown and $10,000 later, we finally gained approval and a reinstated license.

So the moral of the story is:

- Regulators can change the rules at anytime.

- You must be able to pivot quickly to another means of generating income. I was able to secure two private high schools to operate out of at the time.
- Don't get too dependent on just one school (or one course offering).
- If you're in bricks and mortar exclusively, make sure you have at least one spot in a less restrictive area (i.e. county vs. city location) just in case you have to temporarily shut down.

And last but not least. The bigger you are, the harder you fall. Sears Driving School (SDS) was a national driving school brand that was very popular with parents and teens for many years. But, as you're probably familiar, Sears closed its department stores and it was just a matter of time before SDS would shut down. And when they shut down in Texas, they did it almost overnight, leaving over 400 students incomplete in their driver education course. This was approximately $200,000 outstanding services still owed. And the only thing the parents had to draw on for any reimbursement? A $10,000 bond and/or small claims court to gain recompense. Fortunately, other schools stepped up to take the students as transfers but it should serve to remind you that you don't want to ever get yourself too dependent on: another business, one location, one main form of income stream, etc. Always expand slowly, deliberately, weigh the pros and cons, and take calculated risks. Remember, you will always have competition, especially when others see that you're successful. But the way I've always viewed it is that you're your best competition. Always look for ways to improve yourself and your school and you will beat the competition.

Chapter 10: Planning For The Future

What will happen in the future to driver education? Will there always be a need for driving schools? What will happen to your business in the future? What can we do about it, if anything?

These are all relevant questions and must be thought through as a responsible business owner. I knew a school owner that would take a sabbatical annually for two weeks in the winter, close his school down, get away by himself, and think of the best way to operate his school for the upcoming year. It seemed to work for him. Of course, you don't have to go to this extreme but you must take time to think of what the next year holds and how you'll handle any changes.

The future can sometimes be foretold by what's happened in the past. If you've been around as long as I have, you may recall when everyone thought we'd all have flying cars by the turn of the 21st century. No point in learning how to drive cars on the ground if everyone will be flying them, right? .

So what's the next big thing to happen? Autonomous cars? Again, why learn to drive a car if it can drive itself? Surely AI is the answer. It can keep us all safe and reach zero fatalities. At least that's what the makers of these vehicles want us to believe. The problem is that our infrastructure is not set up nationwide for these cars. It will take a long time before everyone will have an autonomous car and it can take them wherever they want to go safely.

There will always be a need for driving schools as long as the public needs to or wants to drive. So long as states mandate a driver education program to be required to take for licensure, and parents want the best training for their teen, there will always be a need.

What will happen to your business in the future? There will be things happen which are out of your control. But you must be able to pivot to survive. Competitors can come in and undercut your tuition. Laws will change. Administrative agencies can change. Gas prices and insurance rates can shoot up almost overnight. You must be prepared for these eventualities and have a backup plan.

What, as school owners, can we do about it, if anything? Follow your state legislature sessions (they meet every two years) and voice your concern over anything that affects your industry. Work with your administrative agency to make sure that all schools are on a level playing field, meaning no one has an advantage over the other, whether big or small. Form a state association and keep active in it. You can get help from a national association such as DSAA (Driving School Association of the Americas) www.dsaa.org.

Be friendly with your competitors. Don't ever get into a price (tuition) war, ever! You'll just hurt yourself and it will be a race to the bottom. Always handle yourself as a professional. The definition of a professional is--Engaged in a specified activity as a career (Webster's). Treat your customers (parents), students (teens and adults), employees (instructors and front office personnel), et al, with respect and expect it in return. Teens can be difficult to deal with at times, but just remember you were a teen at one time too, and it's just a stage that all of us go through. Always conduct yourself ethically and with integrity. As a school owner, you now live life in a fish bowl, and there are some people just waiting for you to say or do the wrong thing. You'll never regret keeping things to yourself that shouldn't be said. Keep learning. There is always something new to learn about your business and industry, marketing, teaching techniques, etc. Share ideas with non-competitor school owners. Some of the best ideas I've gotten were from other owners at national conventions. Don't be afraid to say, "I don't know". Just always add, "But I'll find out and get back to you".

When you become known in your community, you will be sought out by media and other organizations, and you become the "go to" person in your field. You'll then start to be recognized as an SME (Subject Matter Expert). This will also help you to gain more business and recognition, as one feeds off the other. Word of mouth is still the best form of advertising, whether it is in an office setting, neighbor to neighbor, or on an online forum. People trust people they've found trustworthy. And that is your goal in establishing a well run, successful driving school. Remember, that every time you're in the public eye, you represent your school. So always put your right foot forward and you'll never regret it.

Epilogue

In this book, I have attempted to give you, the reader, an all encompassing look at what you need to do to open, run, and have a successful driving school. But as they say, "Even the best laid plans can go awry". And that's the way it is with all small businesses. You can have the best laid business plans with projections showing on paper how successful your business will be. But it's rare that a business survives for 10 years, and unfortunately most don't make it to five. However, I do believe those businesses that have longevity, have an ownership that embraces change, uses it to their advantage, and constantly looks for ways to lead the pack with vision. This doesn't mean that *you* have to be that visionary. There will be others in the driving school industry that will show the way. And if you emulate what they're doing, and change it up (if necessary) to fit your program, you can still lead the way in your business region. This really is the basis of establishing a long term business.

And lastly, I leave you with this: You can do this. It will not be easy. No one ever said it would be. But if you persist, persevere, sell, market, deliver, excel in service, be a people person, keep your nose down and ear to the ground….you will be successful. As long as you offer and deliver value for the money paid, the public will beat a path to your door. Whether be it a storefront or perhaps a virtual one; or maybe even an artificial intelligence clone of yourself in the future.

I do wish you well.

ABOUT THE AUTHOR

Steve Trimble has been in the driver education industry for over 40 years and is a licensed Driver Education Teacher (DET) and a certified Texas DPS Skills Test Examiner. He has facilitated teaching tens of thousands of students in teen driver education, defensive driving, trained instructors, and owned several schools in the greater Houston area. Mr. Trimble holds a Juris Doctorate in law and has been used as an expert witness and consultant on accident/collision and criminal cases. He currently resides in West Houston with his wife and his crazed squirrel chasing dog (borrowed from his daughter) Finn.

If you wish to use my consulting services you can reach me at:
Better Driving Inc.
P.O. Box 6143
Katy, TX. 77491
Or email me at:
betterdriving@peoplepc.com

www.ingramcontent.com/pod-product-compliance
Lightning Source LLC
Chambersburg PA
CBHW071004290526
45795CB00005B/1770